Picnics

o f

Provence

Picnics of Provence

French Country-Style Picnics to Enjoy
At Home or Abroad

Craig Pyes

Paintings by Vincent van Gogh

Simon & Schuster

New York   London   Toronto   Sydney   Tokyo   Singapore

SIMON & SCHUSTER
Simon & Schuster Building
Rockefeller Center
1230 Avenue of the Americas
New York, New York 10020

AN AERO+ASSOCIATES BOOK

Designed by Rita Aero
Map by Cynthia Fitting
Printed in the United States

Separations and Printing by Phoenix Color
Bound by Horowitz/Rae • Production directed by Joanne Barracca

1   3   5   7   9   10   8   6   4   2

Library of Congress Cataloging-in-Publication Data

Pyes, Craig
Picnics of Provence : French country-style picnics to enjoy at home or abroad / Craig Pyes ; paintings by Vincent van Gogh.
p.   cm.
1. Cookery, French—Provençal style. 2. Picnicking. I. Gogh, Vincent van, 1853–1890. II. Title.
TX719.2.P75P84   1993
647.95449—dc20   92-13109
                                                   CIP
ISBN 0-671-78536-2

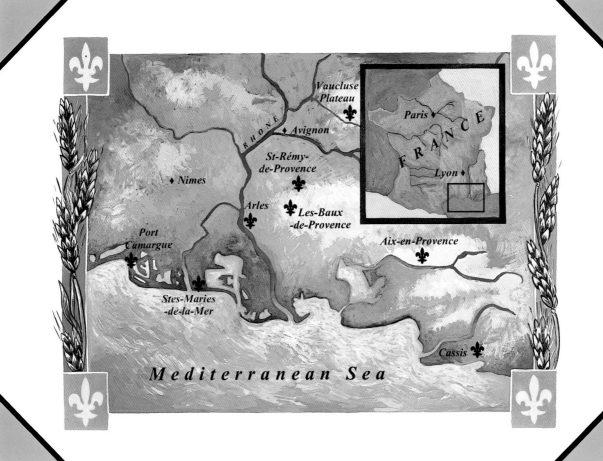

CONTENTS

~ 11 ~

Introduction to French Country-Style Picnics

~ 16 ~

Van Gogh's Market Feast at Arles

Salade Rouge et Verte *(cooked red pepper and asparagus salad)*

Saucisson d'Arles *(regional salami)* on Baguettes with Sliced Tomatoes and Cornichons *(small green pickles)*

Ume-Boshi *(Japanese salted plums)*

Orchard-Fresh Peaches, Plums, Pears, and Apricots

Côtes de Provence Rosé *(chilled wine of the region)*

~ 22 ~

Picnic of Plenty at St-Rémy-de-Provence

Le Grand Aïoli *(garlic mayonnaise)* Feast with Salt Cod, Garden Vegetables, and Hard-boiled Eggs

Citrus Fruits and Fresh Almonds

Bellet *(white or rosé wine from Nice)*

Chocolate-covered Espresso Beans

~ 28 ~

Starry Night Supper at Les Baux-de-Provence

Ratatouille *(cold stew of Provençal vegetables and herbs)*

Gigot d'Agneau *(cold roast leg of lamb)* with Baguettes

Coteaux des Baux-de-Provence *(red wine of the region)*

Platter of Assorted Goat Cheeses

Basket of Purple Grapes

~ 34 ~

Gypsy-Style Banquet at Stes-Maries-de-la-Mer

Tabouleh *(couscous salad)*

Mixed Grill of Fresh Sardines and Sausages with Persillade *(garlic and parsley sauce)*

Roasted Baguettes

Vin de Pays *(red table wine)*

Pastèque Ivre *(watermelon with spirits)*

Campfire Cookout Among the Wild Horses of the Camargue

Seasonal Vegetables and Crudités with Pebrado *(peppered olive oil)* and Aïoli *(garlic mayonnaise)*

Crusty Baguettes Spread with Catoun *(pureé of grilled eggplant)* and Anchouiado *(anchovy paste)*

Grasihado de Peis *(grilled fish flavored with fresh sage)*

Coteaux d'Aix-en-Provence *(chilled white wine)*

Vineigra *(sheep cheese)* with Peaches and Almonds

~ 46 ~

Fish and Loaves Brunch at the Sea Cove of Cassis

Crudités de Céleri *(fresh celery)* with Chèvre Persillade *(goat cheese with garlic and parsley)*

Pan Bagnat *("bathed" sandwich niçoise)*

Cassis Vin Blanc *(white wine of the region)*

Fresh Currant–filled Cantaloupe à la Crème de Cassis

Chocolate Truffles

~ 52 ~

Summer Morning Stroll and Breakfast Picnic at Aix-en-Provence

Prosciutto and Melons de Cavaillon

Muscat de Beaumes-de-Venise *(sweet white wine of the region)*

Omelettes Froids aux Epinards *(cold spinach omelettes)*

Plateau des Fromages and Ficelles *(cheese assortment with small baguettes)*

Croissants aux Amandes *(pastry with almond paste)*

~ 58 ~

Autumn Hunters' Lunch on the Vaucluse Plateau

Pâté with Truffles and Pain de Campagne *(peasant bread)*

Lapin en Papillote *(rabbit cooked in foil)*

Salade Frisée et Chèvre à l'Huile *(curly endive salad with marinated goat cheese)* and Toasted Baguette

Côtes du Luberon and Côtes de Ventoux *(red wines of the region)*

Poached Spiced Pears

An Introduction to French Country-Style Picnics

Having lived in Paris and returned to the United States, I often find myself seized by a nostalgia for France that can be momentarily recaptured by re-creating its cuisine. The food, culture, and geography of France are completely interwoven. As you travel through the country, the names of the towns recall regional delicacies as often as historical sites. Drive past Bresse, and you instantly think of its pampered, grain-fed chickens; stop in Cavaillon, and you conjure up the taste of cool, sweet melons.

Many of us dream of a vacation in Provence. The Provençal lifestyle has become a collective fantasy for millions in the modern world who are weary of urban work schedules, fast food, and supermarkets filled with bright tasteless produce. But if a getaway to Provence is out of the question right now, why not bring Provence to you? *Picnics of Provence* is designed to transport you and your guests on an authentic Provençal outing in the imagined countryside of the south of France. Each of the eight picnics offers a menu that re-creates the flavor and ambience of a special locale.

Your gastronomic journey begins in Arles in late spring among the fruit orchards just as they begin to produce. You will visit St-Rémy-de-Provence for a Grand Aïoli Feast, dine under the stars at romantic Les Baux, and cook over an open fire in the wild terrain of the Camargue. You move on to Stes-Maries-de-la-Mer just in time for the annual Gypsy festival, pass a lazy summer afternoon in a secluded Mediterranean cove at Cassis, and indulge in a morning hike and breakfast picnic at sunny Aix-en-Provence. Your journey concludes in autumn on the Vaucluse highlands soaking up the last bit of warmth among the pine, rosemary, and lavender.

Those who travel through the Provençal countryside soon discover its gastronomic treasures, all available in lively outdoor markets: the cold-pressed olive oil from Maussane-les-Alpilles near Les Baux; the best eating olives from Nyons; the melons from Cavaillon, the cherries of the Vaucluse, lamb that has been grazed on the lavender and thyme of the slopes of the Luberon; the robust wine of Châteauneuf-du-Pape that comes from hillside vineyards once cultivated by the Popes of Avignon.

The cuisine of Provence is light, distinctive in flavor, and among the healthiest diets in the world. The use of aromatics and marinades supplants heavy sauces. Butter is replaced by olive oil, to which is added mild garlic and the wild herbs that grow profusely throughout the region. Many dishes can be enjoyed either hot or cold. And the preferred manner of cooking fish, meat, and even pizza is to grill them over a wood fire — ideal for alfresco meals.

I have selected recipes that both highlight regional flavors and are suitable for outdoor dining. Provençal ingredients — cheeses, pâté, sausage, bread, wines, and condiments — are widely available at gourmet grocery stores in most areas of the States. When you are selecting your fresh produce — the foundation of Provençal cooking — look for home-grown or organic fruits and vegetables, which tend to have more intense flavors. All of the picnics are designed to serve four people, so you'll want to shop accordingly for larger or smaller parties.

To get started on your picnic, you need only a minimum of equipment: a basket to hold the dishes, silverware, food, and napkins; and a tablecloth or ground cover to set them on. You will also need a variety of sealed containers to transport prepared and moist foods, and a sharp knife for cutting meats and bread. Because you are creating a French country picnic, each menu suggests a regional wine to accompany the meal. Don't forget the corkscrew and the wineglasses — wine tastes so much better served in a glass. You may wish to bring along other beverages, such as water, fruit juice, or tea, which are not included in the menus. Since picnics take place in the warmer months, it is a good idea to bring along a cooler to hold perishable foods, fruit, and white wines. Take special care with dishes containing raw egg: Prepare recipes such as aïoli on the day of your picnic and keep them chilled until served.

In each Provençal picnic, I have made suggestions for selecting an outdoor site that will help capture the essence of the picnic's theme or location. You will also find ideas for simple decorations and for activities and entertainments you can enjoy after the meal. No matter how you choose to greet the elements, you'll find that a picnic turns any outing into a holiday. It opens up time to enjoy both food and friends, and adds a touch of majesty even to simple foods like sausage, cheese, and baguettes. French picnics, as a rule, tend to be simple affairs — little more than a jug of wine, a loaf of bread, and thou. French literature is filled with glorious descriptions of elegant afternoons spent *sur l'herbe*, with gastronomic delicacies transported in an antique Louis Vuitton hamper, served on a table dressed in damask, and set under a tree, with glistening ice buckets cradling vintage wines and champagnes.

The van Gogh paintings that illustrate this volume were painted by the artist during his brief but eventful sojourn to Provence during 1888 and 1889. Although the individual works do not always correspond geographically to each picnic site, if you look intently, you will see Provence in them: The sun is strong, the air is fragrant, and there is just a touch of uncertainty created by the threat of a mistral that can hurl down off the mountains in sudden fury and sweep through the Valley of the Rhône.

T*he ancient town of Arles, founded by Julius Caesar, is nestled in the fertile juncture of the Grand and Petit Rhônes. On the outskirts lies van Gogh's "studio" —*

immense meadows of buttercups, ditches lined with purple irises, rows of nodding yellow sunflowers. The dappled emerald Rhône flows through Arles, changing to rich blue in the countryside, where gaily colored fruit orchards give way to burnished, sun-drenched fields of wheat rustling loud as cicadas —

Vaucluse
Plateau

RHÔNE

Avignon

St-Rémy-
de-Provence

Nîmes

Arles

Les-Baux
-de-Provence

Aix-en-Provence

Port
Camargue

Stes-Maries
-de-la-Mer

Cassis

Mediterranean Sea

Van Gogh's Market Feast at Arles

In Arles, the open-air farmers' market springs to life every Saturday along Boulevard des Lices, just outside the old city wall. There, among the hawkers and hagglers, the colorful harvest of Provence bombards the senses. At one end of the market are stalls filled with earth-toned spices and piles of aromatic *herbes de Provence.* Nearby are casks of glistening black Nyons olives; pyramids of red and yellow tomatoes; trays of green, purple, and white asparagus; and artichokes pouring forth in lavender and violet. Farther along are baskets of strawberries; geometries of local goat cheeses set on straw mats; *tellines* (shellfish marinated in wine, garlic, and parsley); chickens roasting on spits; and cages of ducks, roosters, and guinea hens squawking at the fate that awaits them. Shoppers fill their string bags from this seasonal harvest, then stroll to nearby parks or venture to the outskirts of town to picnic in the sun.

Salade Rouge et Verte *(cooked red pepper and asparagus salad)*

Saucisson d'Arles *(regional salami)* on Baguettes with Sliced Tomatoes and Cornichons *(small green pickles)*

Ume-Boshi *(Japanese salted plums)*

Orchard-Fresh Peaches, Plums, Pears, and Apricots

Côtes de Provence Rosé *(chilled wine of the region)*

Preparing Your Market Feast

Your picnic begins the day before with a trip to your local farmers' market to shop for seasonal fresh fruits and vegetables. The night before, you will prepare the pepper and asparagus salad, but all other ingredients will be packed in your basket and prepared at the picnic site. Plan to pick up freshly baked baguettes in the morning.

SALADE ROUGE ET VERTE: Prepare this colorful salad the evening before your outing. Place three whole red bell peppers in a preheated 400 degree oven for about fifteen minutes, or until the skins begin to blister. Enclose the peppers in a paper bag for ten minutes to steam and loosen the skin, then peel, core, and seed the peppers, and cut them into three-quarter-inch strips. Place the peppers in a baking dish and toss with one chopped garlic clove, three tablespoons of extra-virgin olive oil, and a pinch of hot red pepper flakes. Bake, covered, at 400 degrees for forty minutes. Remove the cover and continue baking for another twenty minutes, or until the peppers are slightly charred. Transfer the peppers and cooking juices to a large shallow bowl and let cool.

Meanwhile, steam one pound of whole asparagus until *al dente*, then plunge the asparagus into cold water to stop the cooking. Pat the asparagus dry and add to the bowl of red peppers. Mix in two tablespoons of red wine vinegar, and salt and pepper to taste. Chill overnight in a sealed container that you can pack in your picnic basket the next day.

SAUCISSON D'ARLES ON BAGUETTES WITH SLICED TOMATOES AND CORNICHONS: Across the street from van Gogh's hotel in Arles was a scene he immortalized in his painting

A Pork Butcher's Shop Seen from a Window. Hanging in the butcher shop are *saucissons d'Arles*, the prized local salami. Although *saucisson d'Arles* is not exported, there are several good French salamis available in gourmet stores. One choice is the *saucisson aux herbes de Provence*, which captures the color and aroma of the Arles market. It is made of pork and beef, aged in Beaujolais, and covered with Provençal herbs (fennel, thyme, marjoram, and rosemary).

Pack the *saucisson* in your basket along with several large tomatoes and a container of cornichons. Don't forget to pack a sharp knife. On the morning of your picnic, stop by the bakery and pick up two freshly baked baguettes for the sandwiches. When you're ready to eat, cut the baguettes into sandwich lengths and slice halfway open. Fill with thin slices of *saucisson* and slices of tomato. Serve tangy cornichon pickles on the side.

UME-BOSHI: Influenced by Japanese print artists like Hokusai, van Gogh saw images of Japan in the countryside of Arles. "A little town surrounded by fields all covered with yellow and purple flowers," he wrote to his brother Theo. "Exactly — can't you see it? — like a Japanese dream!" The *ume-boshi* will add a touch of Japan to your Arles market feast. Available in Japanese specialty shops, *ume-boshi* are tiny ripe plums that have been salted and dried. Tantalizingly sweet and briny, they may be savored as a condiment between courses.

ORCHARD-FRESH PEACHES, PLUMS, PEARS, AND APRICOTS: At the first hint of spring, the famous fruit orchards encircling Arles burst into bloom. So moved was van Gogh by this spectacle that he produced fourteen orchard paintings within one month. Fill your picnic basket with summer fruits to celebrate the colorful bounty of the orchards: creamy pink peaches, bright purple plums, yellow-green pears, and pale golden apricots. Pack a small sharp paring knife for each guest.

CÔTES DE PROVENCE ROSÉ: A golden pink rosé is the wine of choice for this Provençal country sojourn. Côtes de Provence is known principally for its rosé wines, but the neighboring apellations of Tavel and Brandol make excellent substitutes. Another very good choice is the rosé from Domaine Ott, although it may be expensive and difficult to find. Chill the wine overnight and pack it in your basket just before you leave.

Staging Your Market Feast

One last stop on the way to your picnic site should be the *fleuriste*, where you will choose flowers to decorate your picnic spread. Select from giant sunflowers, purple irises, or branches of fruit blossoms. If it is May Day, buy lilies of the valley to affix to each guest's lapel.

Choose your van Gogh picnic spot with an eye to his unique artistic vision: perhaps the town park (*The Poets' Garden*), or a nearby farm (*Wheat Field at the Foot of the Alpilles*), or within view of a favorite scenic spot (*Langlois Bridge*). Once you've found the perfect site, spread your blanket and arrange the flowers you've brought along. After you've enjoyed the taste and color of your lunch — vibrant with the red and green of the salad, and shaded with the rich pastels of the fresh fruit — you may want to indulge in a uniquely van Gogh experience. Maybe you've brought along a sketch pad for each guest and a large box of French oil pastels. Now, you may wile away the afternoon rendering a still life of the picnic scene you've created, sketching the nearby landscape, or creating impressionist portraits of one another.

The small medieval town of St-Rémy-de-Provence stands at the gateway to the Alpilles chain, seventeen miles to the northeast of Arles. Its environs are lush with fruit orchards and vegetable gardens, flowering almond trees, ancient olive groves, and twisted cypresses. To the south of town is the asylum of St-Paul-de-Mausole, where van Gogh retreated after his stay in Arles. Beyond that, in a gladed trough at the base of the jagged foothills, are the Greco-Roman ruins of Glanum, like exposed roots growing out of the past.

Vaucluse Plateau

RHONE

Avignon

St-Rémy-de-Provence

Nîmes

Arles

Les-Baux-de-Provence

Port Camargue

Aix-en-Provence

Stes-Maries-de-la-Mer

Cassis

Mediterranean Sea

Picnic of Plenty at St-Rémy-de-Provence

St-Rémy has everything people dream of in a Provençal town, from its medieval heart to its lively outdoor cafes, pleasant fountains, and bustling markets displaying produce from the small farms and gardens that surround it. The dry, breezy air is perfumed with the aromatic herbs that form the essence of Provençal cuisine.

St-Rémy has long been known for its sumptuous feasts. One, described by a native son — the sixteenth-century clairvoyant Nostradamus — had fifteen courses, including ten kinds of fowl, roasted piglets, and whole kids served to each guest on a silver platter. To this day, people from the countryside continue to gather for summer festivals, where they blend the harvest fresh from the fields with the elixir of garlic to create the Provençal smorgasbord of *Le Grand Aïoli*.

Le Grand Aïoli (*garlic mayonnaise)* Feast with Salt Cod, Garden Vegetables,
and Hard-boiled Eggs

Citrus Fruits and Fresh Almonds

Bellet *(white or rosé wine from Nice)*

Chocolate-covered Espresso Beans

Preparing your Picnic of Plenty

Le Grand Aïoli Feast, or the *Aïoli Monstre*, is a traditional Provençal picnic of plenty — an expandable feast. The centerpiece is a bowl of tangy garlic mayonnaise in which to dip salt cod, hard-boiled eggs, and cooked and fresh vegetables. Shop early the day before your picnic for the vegetables and fruits you will need. Chocolate espresso beans are available at coffee stores. Dried salt cod can be found at Italian groceries and should be purchased two days before your picnic. Boneless salt cod has less salt and can be soaked overnight, but the dried cod with bones is saltier and must be soaked for twenty-four hours.

LE GRAND AÏOLI: Prepare this zesty garlic mayonnaise on the morning of your picnic. You can make it spicy by adding cayenne, vary the flavor with chopped fresh basil, or tone down its pungency by decreasing the amount of garlic.

Press three cloves of garlic into a bowl. With a fork or pestle, mash in a pinch of salt and blend in one large egg yolk. Measure one cup of virgin olive oil. Add a few drops of the oil to the egg yolk mixture, and whisk vigorously until the mixture thickens to the consistency of mayonnaise. Whisk in the rest of the oil a tablespoonful at a time, until it is completely blended into the mixture. (Note: The egg yolk and oil must be at room temperature for the mayonnaise to emulsify.) When you've finished, blend in a squeeze of lemon juice. Taste and add salt, if necessary. Transfer the aïoli to a picnic container, cover, and refrigerate until you are ready to leave.

SALT COD: Salt cod, a dried fish, is the centerpiece of the aïoli feast. Purchase about one pound of boneless salt cod and soak it overnight by covering the fish with water in a shallow baking dish and placing it in the refrigerator. If you can find only the saltier cod with bones, soak it for twenty-four hours, changing the water at least four times during this time period to reduce the salt content.

On the morning of your picnic, drain the fish and transfer it to a skillet. Cover the cod with fresh water and bring to a boil. Immediately, remove the pan from the heat and let it cool to room temperature. Drain the fish, clean away the bones and skin, and break the fish into large pieces for dipping. Wrap the fish pieces and chill them in the refrigerator until you are ready to leave.

GARDEN VEGETABLES AND HARD-BOILED EGGS: The traditional garden vegetables used in a Grand Aïoli Feast include carrots, beets, tiny new potatoes, cauliflower, and green beans. You may select other fresh vegetables in season, and vary the presentation with both cooked and fresh vegetables.

You can prepare the vegetables and eggs the night before your picnic, so that they will be thoroughly chilled before you pack them. Boil the whole beets and whole new potatoes in their skins for thirty minutes, or until just tender. If you wish, parboil the green beans and cauliflower until slightly tender. Trim the cooked and fresh vegetables into dipping-size pieces. Leave the potatoes whole. Wrap the vegetables and refrigerate them for several hours or overnight.

Hard boil the eggs, one for each guest. Leave them in their shells and refrigerate for several hours or overnight.

CITRUS FRUITS AND FRESH ALMONDS: The perfect conclusion to Le Grand Aïoli Feast is the clean and invigorating taste of citrus. Pack your basket with a selection of ripe tangerines, juicy naval oranges, bright red blood oranges, and sweet pink grapefruit. Also pack a large bag of whole raw (unroasted) almonds to eat along with the citrus. Don't forget to bring a sharp knife to cut the larger fruits.

BELLET: There is no agreement on the best wine to consume with the aïoli, but a chilled Bellet from Nice — white or rosé — has the vote of a number of locals. The wine is dry and flinty, with just a touch of fruit. Look for a Château de Cremat from Charles Bagnis.

CHOCOLATE-COVERED ESPRESSO BEANS: After your guests are thoroughly sated with Le Grand Aïoli, pass around the chocolate-covered espresso beans to take away the taste of garlic and to stimulate their spirits.

Staging Your Picnic of Plenty

The Aïoli Feast can be enjoyed in the countryside or on the lawn or in the garden just outside your home. Begin and end the meal like the sixteenth-century guests at Nostradamus' grand feast: Sprinkle rose water over one another's hands. If the picnic is small, place the bowl of aïoli in the center, and arrange the vegetables and fish on platters. If you intend to invite the whole village, then put the aïoli in multiple bowls and place the platters of food in the center. After you finish your citrus and almonds, nibble just a few more espresso beans, and perhaps sample another sip of Bellet, you may want to try and foretell the future as Nostradamus did. And yes, he predicted you

The commanding rocky heights of Les Baux float like an island off the southern flanks of the Alpilles, an arid limestone chain whose saw-toothed peaks cut through the heart of Provence between Avignon and Arles. The crumbling fortress town, perched on sheer escarpments plunging precipitously on all sides, is best approached from the north, coming from St-Rémy. By that route you will pass near the rocky cataclysm of the Val d'Enfer, the evil-looking gorge whose mysterious grottoes inspired Dante's Amphitheater of Hell.

Starry Night Supper at Les Baux-de-Provence

At the edge of the village of Les Baux, the twisted ruins of an ancient castle assume fantastic shapes in the moonlight, evoking its history of love and menace. During the Middle Ages Les Baux gained renown for its Courts of Love. Poets came from all over to compose and sing passionate verses idealizing the noble ladies. Under the stars, supper was served to the enchanted gatherings.

Although the desolate eyrie — once home to warring nobles, wandering troubadours, and murderous brigands — has collapsed into heaps of rock and ruin, on summer nights the tradition continues. Groups enter the ruins with with food-filled baskets. Platters are set out, candles are lit, and the eventide is passed in wine and song. Lights from small farmhouses twinkle in the distance, and the night sky is bright with stars.

Ratatouille *(cold stew of Provençal vegetables and herbs)*

Gigot d'Agneau *(cold roast leg of lamb)* with Baguettes

Coteaux des Baux-de-Provence *(red wine of the region)*

Platter of Assorted Goat Cheeses

Basket of Purple Grapes

Preparing Your Starry Night Supper

The day before the Starry Night Supper, shop for the meat, produce, and cheeses you will need. Plan to cook the ratatouille and lamb on the morning of your evening outing. The ratatouille becomes especially fragrant and tasty after spending the day in repose. On the day of your picnic, pick up two baguettes at the bakery. They will accompany the ratatouille and goat cheeses, and can be used to make sandwiches of the lamb.

RATATOUILLE: This popular Provençal dish of local vegetables and herbs is delicious served hot or cold. There are numerous variations of the recipe, but it is best when the shapes and flavors of the vegetables are preserved.

Remove the skin from one medium eggplant, cut it into one-inch thick slices, then quarter the slices into cubes, sprinkle well with salt, and let drain in a colander for thirty minutes. Cut two large zucchini into one-inch slices, sprinkle with salt, and drain along with the eggplant. Core and seed two red bell peppers, cut into cubes, and set aside. Cut four medium tomatoes into eight wedges each and set aside. Dice two onions and chop two cloves of garlic.

While the eggplant and zucchini drain, heat two tablespoons of olive oil in a large skillet over medium heat. Add the onions, garlic, one bay leaf, four whole peppercorns, and one teaspoon of fresh or dried thyme. Cook for ten minutes, or until the onions are translucent. Add the tomatoes and red pepper and cook, covered, another twenty minutes over medium-low heat.

While the sauce is simmering, using another skillet, sauté the zucchini in two tablespoons of

olive oil for about ten minutes and add to the simmering sauce. Repeat with the eggplant. Stir the ratatouille and let it simmer, covered, another ten to fifteen minutes. Salt and pepper to taste. Remove to a bowl, cover, and refrigerate the ratatouille for the remainder of the day.

When you are ready to leave, remove the bay leaf from the ratatouille and stir in the juice of one lemon. Transfer to your picnic container and sprinkle the top with chopped fresh parsley.

GIGOT D'AGNEAU: Lamb makes an excellent cold dish, just right for a medieval-style picnic. Select a five-pound leg of lamb at your butcher shop (you may substitute the two sirloin halves of a leg). Trim the fat, but leave in the bone. With a sharp knife pierce the meat in several places and insert slivers of garlic. Put the meat in a baking pan, brush with olive oil, salt lightly, and cover with long sprigs of fresh rosemary. Roast in a preheated 375 degree oven for forty-five minutes, or until the meat thermometer reads 130 degrees for rare or 140 degrees for medium rare. When the lamb is done, remove from the oven, discard the rosemary, and allow the meat to cool slightly before refrigerating until evening. When you are ready to go, wrap the meat and pack it in your basket. Bring along a jar of Dijon mustard to daub on the meat.

COTEAUX DES BAUX-DE-PROVENCE: Les Baux has its own appellation, which produces fine red wines that are fruity and well balanced. The wines are frequently exported as Coteaux d'Aix-en-Provence, but Les Baux is a geographically distinct, smaller growing area. Check the label under the appellation to find a wine that comes from Les Baux. An excellent choice is Domaine de Trevallon Les Baux.

PLATTER OF ASSORTED GOAT CHEESES: Include a selection of your favorite goat cheeses to sample after the meal. Select from the many goat cheeses that are available — plain, herbed, peppered, or marinated in olive oil. Let your guests spread the goat cheese on baguettes to eat along with the juicy purple grapes.

BASKET OF PURPLE GRAPES: At the bottom of the sheer cliff face of Les Baux stretch vineyards of dark purple grapes. The soil is said to be especially fertile thanks to the fourteenth-century brigand Raymond de Turenne, who delighted in throwing his prisoners off the castle walls onto the plains where the grapes now grow. Wash and chill the grapes before packing them.

Staging Your Starry Night Supper

At Les Baux, evening picnics occur on moonlit nights so that the guests can find their way. Select a spot out in the open where you have a view of the town lights twinkling on the horizon. Travel back through time and re-create the setting of a medieval *festin*. Instead of plates, pack wooden trenchers for the slices of meat and daubs of mustard, rustic bowls for the ratatouille, oversize goblets for the wine, and unpressed linen napkins for the hands. Bring along many candles to light the table and sharp knives for each guest to cut their meat from the bone. Before and after the meal, set a medieval mood with a traditional hand-washing ceremony: Sprinkle orange water or rose water on one another's hands and dry them on the linen napkins.

Perhaps you've brought along instruments to play after you are thoroughly sated — wooden flutes, tambourines, mandolins, and chimes. Or maybe you've brought poetry to recite as you re-create the magic of a starry night and *l'amour courtois* of medieval Les Baux.

N ear where the Petit Rhône empties into the Mediterranean stands the former fishing village of Stes-Maries-de-la-Mer. As you approach you see the gray stones of the fortified church rising above terra-cotta roofs and cabane-style houses. The sea salt livens the air, and fishermen sit languidly on the jetty listening to the hum of small boats going in and out of the harbor. Then a sudden squall of swallows above the church-bell gable announces the arrival of the Gypsies.

Gypsy-Style Banquet at Stes-Maries-de-la-Mer

The world's most famous gathering of *Rom* takes place on May 24 and 25 at Stes-Maries-de-la-Mer, as thousands of Gypsies assemble for a time of pilgrimage, processions, and open-air feasts. They have come to venerate Sara — their patron saint — whose dark, melancholic effigy, swathed in colored garments, will be carried on their shoulders from her somber crypt to the sun-sparkled sea.

The campgrounds and beaches are filled with music and camp fires as the *voyageurs* honor one another with food, songs, dances, and apocryphal stories. Here you are not rich because you have a fortune, but because you've spent one entertaining. So prepare your camp and turn no one away. The sharing of cooked food symbolizes fellowship. *T'aven baXtale taj saste!* May you be lucky and healthy!

Tabouleh *(couscous salad)*

Mixed Grill of Fresh Sardines and Sausages with Persillade *(garlic and parsley sauce)*

Roasted Baguettes

Vin de Pays *(red table wine)*

Pastèque Ivre *(watermelon with spirits)*

The fish and sausages will be grilled out of doors at your picnic site. The tabouleh and *persillade* should be prepared at home on the morning of your picnic, but the watermelon must be prepared the night before. Shop the day before your picnic for the watermelon, vegetables, fresh herbs, and sausages, which can be found at most specialty butchers. The fish, however, should be purchased the morning of the picnic. On the way to your picnic site, stop by the bakery for fresh baguettes.

TABOULEH: This chilled North African grain dish is a refreshing addition to any picnic. Unlike traditional tabouleh, which calls for bulgur or cracked wheat, the Provençal version uses couscous, made from semolina. Prepare the tabouleh early on the morning of your outing. Pour one cup of instant or quick-cooking couscous into a medium-size bowl and add one-and-a-half cups of cold water. Cover and let the mixture stand until all the water is absorbed, about thirty minutes. Meanwhile, mince one-half cup of fresh parsley and one-half cup of fresh mint leaves. Core, seed, and chop four medium tomatoes. Finely chop six scallions. After thirty minutes, drain any excess water from the couscous and add the chopped ingredients. Mix and fluff the salad with a fork. In a small bowl, mix one-quarter cup of olive oil and the juice of one lemon. Add this dressing to the tabouleh, mix, and add salt and pepper to taste. Refrigerate until you are ready to leave.

MIXED GRILL OF FRESH SARDINES AND SAUSAGES: During the festival at Stes-Maries, the most common sight in the Gypsy camps is smoking grills filled with fresh sardines and local sausages. If possible, buy your fish the morning of your picnic — about a ten-ounce fish for each

guest. If you cannot find fresh sardines, substitute small whole fish such as perch or trout. Wash the fish, pat them dry, and rub them generously inside and out with olive oil. Sprinkle them with salt and pepper and wrap them tightly. Transport the fish to the picnic site in a cooler.

Sausages commonly found in Provence are the Merguez — a thin North African delicacy made of beef, lamb, and hot spices — and cured pork sausages such as *saucissons de Lyon*. A specialty butcher can provide you with these or similar fresh sausages. Buy two small sausages for each guest. Keep the sausages refrigerated until you are ready to leave.

Before placing the meat and fish on the grill, allow the coals to burn down to prevent the fish from sticking to the grill. When you are ready to eat, lay the sausages and fish on the grill together. Cook the sausages until they are well done, and cook the whole fish until the flesh is firm, about five minutes on each side. Place the grilled fish and sausages on a platter, and let your guests debone their own fish and spoon the *persillade* on top.

PERSILLADE: Prepare the persillade on the morning of your picnic. In a small bowl, place a handful of finely chopped parsley and two cloves of crushed garlic. Stir in one-quarter cup of olive oil and add the juice of one-half lemon. Add salt and pepper to taste and seal in a picnic container.

ROASTED BAGUETTES: Immediately after you have removed the fish and sausages from the grill, lay several whole baguettes over the coals. Turn them continuously until they become hot and crusty, about three to four minutes. Let your guests tear off pieces of the hot bread.

VIN DE PAYS: A simple table wine is the right accompaniment to a Gypsy-style cookout, so look for a rustic *vin de pays*, or "country wine," which is generally of decent quality and can be drunk through the night. Domaine de la Gautiere is a good red *vin de pays*. It is fruity and well balanced, with low acid, and it complements grilled foods nicely.

PASTÈQUE IVRE: At the end of a spicy meal, nothing is more refreshing than slices of chilled watermelon. In Provence the watermelons come with red, white, or yellow flesh. Select a small sweet melon for your *pastèque ivre*, or drunken watermelon. The day before your picnic, cut a one-and-a-half-inch hole in the rind. Fill a turkey baster with one-quarter cup of marc de Provence (distilled wine) or grappa. Push the baster into the center of the melon and slowly release the liquor. Reinsert the rind plug, seal with melted wax or plastic tape, and refrigerate overnight.

Staging Your Gypsy-Style Banquet

Knowledge of good stopping places is the key to Gypsy survival. Be sure to select a site where you can lay a cooking fire, and plan your outdoor Gypsy banquet late in the day, so the fires will burn brightly as the sun sets. Why not set up camp in the old way, with a tent or canopy and colorful quilts arranged on the ground? Unpack your dishes — mismatched china is the right look — and let the feast begin. Always start with a toast to those present, but spill the first drops of wine on the ground for the dead. In the Gypsy tradition, toasts accompany every story told to the assembled *phrala* (fellows). Tales are told deep into the night, and every story is true, even if it never happened! Spontaneous outbreaks of singing and dancing may occur, so bring along musical instruments — violin, guitar, cymbalom. And remember, Gypsies carry along their fortune-telling cards wherever they go, just in case some *gaje* happen by.

J ust above the city of Arles, the Petit Rhône forks west from the Grand Rhône, and the river embraces between its two arms the mystical land of black fighting bulls and free white horses, pink flamingos, and enchanting mirages. You are in the Camargue — the Rhône's wild southern delta, and one of Europe's most important wildlife refuges. It is a land ruled by sun, wind, and water. Studded with glasswort and tamarisk, its gleaming lagoons and inland marshes are held from the sea by a fragile littoral of dunes —

Campfire Cookout Among the Wild Horses of the Camargue

At the heart of the Camargue is the Vaccares Lagoon, a great inland sea whose still blue waters tremble with the pulse of beating wings from thousands of migrating birds. Nearby a small family of wild horses grazes. Farther down the shore a herd of black bulls is being watched by the *gardiens*, Camargue cowboys whose long tridents pierce the sky.

Spring is the social season in the Camargue. Great feasts are prepared and celebrated, while small groups of friends venture into the countryside to picnic and search for the wild asparagus that is just sprouting. Freshly caught fish is rubbed with sage and grilled over glowing wood embers. Savory spreads and piquant sauces are eaten with hardy breads and seasonal vegetables. *Bonne biasso!* Eat well!

Seasonal Vegetables and Crudités with Pebrado *(peppered olive oil)* and Aïoli *(garlic mayonnaise)*

Crusty Baguettes Spread with Catoun *(pureé of grilled eggplant)* and Anchouiado *(anchovy paste)*

Grasihado de Peis *(grilled fish flavored with fresh sage)*

Coteaux d'Aix-en-Provence *(chilled white wine)*

Vineigra *(sheep cheese)* with Peaches and Almonds

Preparing Your Camargue Cookout

The sauces and spreads and even the fish can all be prepared at home and packed in your picnic basket. Most of the sauces, however, can be easily prepared at the picnic site. The day before your picnic, shop for the fresh produce and other ingredients you will need. If you can, purchase fresh fish and warm baguettes on the morning of your picnic.

SEASONAL VEGETABLES AND CRUDITÉS: Clean and trim baby asparagus, hearts of celery, baby carrots, fennel, small boiled new potatoes, and mushrooms. The asparagus may be precooked if you wish. Wrap the vegetables tightly and refrigerate until you are ready to go.

PEBRADO: Pack your basket with tiny saucers for the picnickers to prepare their own *pebrado*. Fill the saucers with a fine olive oil from Provence and season to taste with salt and pepper. Pass the celery hearts for your guests to dip into the *pebrado*.

AÏOLI: Make this savory garlic mayonnaise on the morning of your picnic. Press three cloves of garlic into a bowl and mash a pinch of salt into it with a fork. Beat in one large egg yolk. Measure one cup of extra-virgin olive oil and add a few drops of the oil to the egg yolk mixture, stirring vigorously until the mixture thickens. Thoroughly blend in the rest of the oil, a tablespoonful at a time, until it is completely absorbed. (Note: The egg yolk and oil must be at room temperature for the mayonnaise to emulsify.) When you've finished, blend in a squeeze of lemon juice. Taste and add salt, if needed. Put into a small container and chill until you are ready to depart. Aïoli is an excellent accompaniment to vegetables and fish.

CATOUN: If you are building a fire, this tasty eggplant spread may also be made on location. Grill several small whole eggplants over the embers, turning them occasionally until they are charred and wrinkled. (At home, cook them in a very hot oven until the skins are charred.) Peel the eggplant and place the pulp in a bowl. To the warm eggplant, add a clove or two of minced garlic, a handful of chopped fresh parsley, and a drizzle of olive oil. Mash and blend the mixture with a fork. Add salt and pepper to taste. At your picnic site, spread the *catoun* on slices of crusty baguette.

ANCHOUIADO: This flavorful anchovy paste is also simple to prepare at your picnic site. Drain a jar (or two) of anchovy fillets and place them on a plate. Using a fork, mash them with a few drops of olive oil, a squirt of lemon juice, and some freshly ground pepper. *Anchouiado*, too, is spread on slices of baguette.

GRASIHADO DE PEIS: Carp, mullet, mackerel, bass, cod, and eel are among the wide variety of fish you'll find on a typical Camargue cookout. Select a large whole fish, wash and pat it dry, and slip a sprig of fresh sage inside. Baste the fish with *pebrado* and grill over the coals of a wood fire. Every once in a while throw a handful of fresh sage on the fire and let it smoke into the fish. Baste while cooking, turn the fish once, and cook until the flesh is firm, about twenty to thirty minutes. The fish may be prepared at home by baking it for thirty to forty minutes on sprigs of sage in a preheated 350 degree oven and basting it with *pebrado*. You can cook the fish just before you leave, or even the day before, and serve it cold.

COTEAUX D'AIX-EN-PROVENCE: A light dry white wine is the ideal accompaniment to this picnic. The Camargue is not a wine region, but try a white Coteaux d'Aix-en-Provence or a dry white from Cassis. Chill the wine before you pack it; it need be only slightly cool when served.

VINEIGRA WITH PEACHES AND ALMONDS: You may be hard-pressed to find the sheep cheese of the Camargue known as *vineigra*, but any fresh sheep cheese can be substituted. Also pack ripe peaches and raw almonds in your basket. As you nibble them for dessert let them bring to mind the blossoming fruit and nut trees in Languedoc and the Petite Camargue just to the west.

Staging Your Camargue Cookout

Camargue picnickers venture cross-country with their baskets of food and blankets before settling on a picnic site. As they go, they see bulrushes studded with nests holding speckled eggs of all colors and sizes. While you might not see great white Russian swans winging toward their dense northern forests, or a flock of flamingos with their long necks outstretched, you'll want to bring along binoculars and a field guide for bird watching.

45
↩

To really experience a Camargue-style outing, select a location where you can build a cooking fire. When you've found the perfect spot with just a bit of shade, unfurl your blankets and prepare for an afternoon of outdoor delights. If the day is warm, you may want to linger until the sunset glows across the landscape. But keep an eye open. The *gardiens* of the Camargue know that even in the best of weather they must consult the sky. That sudden sea breeze could signal an east wind, which will darken the skies, make the waters rise, and send nervous whinnies through the horse herd. There is nothing to do then but add wood to the campfire and huddle together.

H

eading toward the Riviera along the storm-battered Mediterranean coast between Marseilles and Toulon, the road twists along severe stone-faced cliffs rising from the sea. The first stop is the tiny fishing port of Cassis, one of the small coastal towns and secluded bays you will find along the way. Above its crescent harbor, olives, figs, and grape ripen in the hills. At the town's outskirts, deep inlets cut into the escarpments, yielding tiny slivers of white sun-soaked sandy beaches.

Vaucluse Plateau

RHONE

♦ Avignon

St-Rémy-de-Provence

♦ Nimes

Arles

Les-Baux-de-Provence

Aix-en-Provence

Port Camargue

Stes-Maries-de-la-Mer

Cassis

Mediterranean Sea

Fish and Loaves Brunch at the Sea Cove of Cassis

"He who has seen Paris but has not seen Cassis has seen nothing," wrote the Provençal poet Frederic Mistral. The charming port town, with its eighteenth-century buildings overlooking colorful fishing boats bobbing in the sea, has long been a popular summer resort for French artists. Its restaurants and sidewalk cafes teem with people in relaxed conversation, eating bouillabaisse made from the day's catch, and washing it down with the spicy white wine of Cassis.

Just out of town, fingers of land jut into the sea forming the stony walls of *calanques*, the Mediterranean version of Norwegian fjords. Far below the jagged, pine-spotted ridges, clear azure waters slap lazily onto a small beach — a perfect spot for wading, boating, probing a secret fishing spot, and eating out of doors.

Crudités de Céleri *(fresh celery)* with Chèvre Persillade *(goat cheese with garlic and parsley)*

Pan Bagnat *("bathed" sandwich niçoise)*

Cassis Vin Blanc *(white wine of the region)*

Fresh Currant–filled Cantaloupe à la Crème de Cassis

Chocolate Truffles

Preparing Your Cassis Brunch

The day before your picnic, shop for the produce you will need — celery, tomatoes, onions, bell peppers, parsley, currants, and cantaloupe. Chill the fruits and vegetables overnight. The Fish and Loaves Brunch is a spontaneous, rustic meal that requires only simple preparation on the morning of your picnic. Much of it is assembled at the picnic site, which is a Provençal entertainment in itself.

CRUDITÉS DE CÉLERI WITH CHÈVRE PERSILLADE: Separate and wash one bunch of celery, wrap the stalks tightly, and refrigerate until you are ready to leave.

To prepare the goat cheese spread, begin with a basic *persillade*. In a small bowl, place a handful of finely chopped parsley and one clove of crushed garlic. Add three tablespoons of olive oil, one tablespoon of lemon juice, and a dash of freshly ground pepper. Mix and add one soft eight-ounce fresh goat cheese. Mix the goat cheese into the *persillade* mixture until it is completely blended. Pack this spread into a picnic container and chill along with the celery stalks.

Serve this as a first course while you prepare the *pan bagnat*. Let your guests spread their own stalks of celery with the chèvre and *persillade*.

PAN BAGNAT: This is traditional picnic fare in Provence — a sandwich "bathed" in olive oil. It is basically a *salade niçoise* made portable on a round platter of bread. Pack your picnic basket with one can of solid white tuna packed in water, four hard-boiled eggs, a small jar of capers, a can of anchovy filets, several cloves of garlic, and a small bottle of olive oil. For the basic sandwich filling you will also need one Bermuda onion, cut into thin rings; four tomatoes, thinly

sliced; and one red bell pepper and one green bell pepper sliced into thin rings. Also bring along salt and pepper, and a sharp knife. On the way to your picnic site, stop by the bakery and pick up four small round loaves of peasant bread about six inches in diameter.

When you're ready to make your sandwiches, peel several cloves of garlic and slice them in half. Open the can of anchovy filets and drain them. Open the can of tuna and drain. Peel the hardboiled eggs and cut each into four long wedges. Slice each small loaf of bread in half through the middle to form a sandwich. Rub the insides of the bread with the cut garlic. Drizzle about one tablespoon of olive oil on each side of the bread and lightly salt and pepper. In each sandwich, pile on slices of onion, tomato, and bell pepper, and sprinkle on a few capers. Top the vegetables with two or three anchovy filets, pieces of crumbled tuna, and wedges of hard-boiled egg. Put the sandwich together and squish it down. *Pan bagnat* is very filling and quite tasty. The sandwich should be moist and messy, which is why Provençal wisdom suggests it should be eaten at the beach. After all, it is called *pan bagnat* — a "bathed" sandwich.

CASSIS VIN BLANC: Look for a local white wine of Cassis, which is truly a small wine that has made it big. The Nobel Prize–winning Provençal poet Mistral wrote of this wine in *Calendu:* "It gleams like a limpid diamond. It smells of rosemary, heather, and myrtle. It dances in the glass." What makes it so dry and jaunty is that it is grown in the chalky soil of the terraced rocky slopes overlooking the Mediterranean in the full glory of the sun. Chill the wine until you are ready to leave.

FRESH CURRANT–FILLED CANTALOUPE À LA CRÈME DE CASSIS: On the morning of your picnic, halve and seed two chilled cantaloupes, then put the halves together and wrap tightly. Pack the cantaloupe in your basket along with a pound of fresh currants removed from the stem (fresh blueberries or raspberries can be substituted), and a small bottle of *crème de cassis* liqueur.

After the hardy *pan bagnat* has been consumed, and before you've started your outdoor nap, you'll want to serve the refreshing cantaloupe. Fill a half cantaloupe with fresh currants (or berries) for each guest. Drizzle a little dark purple *crème de cassis* over the currants.

CHOCOLATE TRUFFLES: The day before your picnic, shop at a confectionery for fine chocolate truffles. Truffles are made in many flavors, and you may wish to purchase an assortment. Keep the truffles refrigerated until it is time to leave. They should be served slightly chilled, so keep them in your cooler at your picnic site. They make a delightful pick-me-up after a seaside nap.

Staging Your Cassis Brunch

On weekends, French picnickers gather their ingredients — the young goat cheeses of the region, the fine breads, the ripe produce at the farmers' market — and drift toward the seashore. To capture the ambience of a Cassis picnic, find your own secluded beach or a setting near water, perhaps with a view of boats or with the possibility of fishing. Set up your camp — no cooking required here — then head for the water. If you've brought along fishing tackle, find that secluded spot hidden among the rocks, and wait for the ingredients of a future bouillabaisse to strike the line. Or, lay back and practice the fine art of the outdoor nap. As you can plainly see, this indulgent brunch is designed for fishing and loafing.

A few miles north of Marseilles and the Mediterranean coast is Aix-en-Provence, the old regional capital, built in the great basin just west of the luminescent limestone canvas of Mt. Ste-Victoire. Everywhere in this genteel town you are reminded of the grace born from the interplay of space and light, from its elegant seventeenth- and eighteenth-century mansions, to its broad sun-dappled avenues lined with plane trees and sidewalk cafes, to its gurgling fountains and intimate squares that invite passersby to pause —

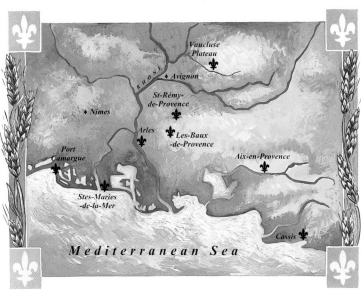

Summer Morning Stroll and Breakfast Picnic at Aix-en-Provence

A day in Aix is certain to begin or end in one of its many outdoor cafes, such as Les Deux Garçons situated on the Cours Mirabeau, which many consider to be the most beautiful main street in Europe, if not the world. Throughout the day, people promenade under the cool canopy of the plane trees, stop for a *café crème*, listen to the splashing fountains, and marvel at the limpidity of the light.

After the first cup of coffee, but well before the morning sun gets too high, breakfast picnickers depart for their favorite spots on the slopes of nearby Mt. Ste-Victoire. Many explore the dark green woods above the Zola Dam; some hike east to the crest overlooking the five-hundred-foot-deep Garagai Chasm; others breakfast at Croix de Provence at the summit.

Prosciutto and Melons de Cavaillon

Muscat de Beaumes-de-Venise *(sweet white wine of the region)*

Omelettes Froids aux Epinards *(cold spinach omelettes)*

Plateau des Fromages and Ficelles *(cheese assortment with small baguettes)*

Croissants aux Amandes *(pastry with almond paste)*

The day before the picnic, shop for the cheeses, wine, prosciutto, and melons. You will need fresh spinach and eggs for the omelettes, which will be prepared the morning of your picnic. On the way to your picnic site, stop at a bakery and pick up the croissants and *ficelles* (small baguettes).

PROSCIUTTO AND MELONS DE CAVAILLON: This classic combination adds a simple elegance to any meal. While prosciutto comes from nearby Italy, it has long been assimilated into the culture of Provence. You will need one-quarter pound of this flavorful ham, cut into paper-thin slices so that it is nearly transparent. If you can find it, splurge on imported *prosciutto di Parma.* Wrap it tightly and refrigerate overnight.

According to the French, the best of all possible melons come from Cavaillon in Provence. The Cavaillon variety is a small, pale green melon with sweet orange flesh, first harvested in May and continuing through the summer. Although the Cavaillon melon enjoys worldwide renown, its distribution has not kept up with its reputation. If you cannot find it, substitute honeydew melon, a distant cousin by taste. You'll need about two pounds.

Refrigerate the melon overnight. On the morning of your picnic, seed the melon, cut it into thin wedges, and remove the rinds. Wrap the wedges together and refrigerate until you are ready to go. If you wish, you may cut the chilled melon at your picnic site. Begin your breakfast picnic by letting your guests wrap slices of prosciutto around the bite-sized wedges of cool, fragrant melon.

MUSCAT DE BEAUMES-DE-VENISE: The King René Fountain at the end of the Cours

Mirabeau commemorates the king's introduction of the deliciously sweet Muscat grape to Provence during his reign in the fifteenth century. The vines, which have since been cultivated in the foothills of the Dentelles, produce a sweet wine that makes a perfect accompaniment for prosciutto and melon. Refrigerate the wine overnight, then remove it the morning of your picnic so it will be very slightly chilled when served.

OMELETTES FROIDS AUX EPINARDS: Cold vegetable omelettes cooked in olive oil are a traditional picnic food in Provence. They are often served as a light first course to a larger meal, or packed into haversacks to eat while hiking. Each omelette requires three eggs and one-half pound of fresh spinach, so shop accordingly.

Wash the spinach carefully and discard the stems. Parboil it for three minutes, drain it in a colander, and squeeze out all the remaining water with a fork or spoon. Coarsely chop the cooked spinach on a cutting board. Make each omelette separately. Heat one tablespoon of olive oil in an omelette pan over medium-low heat. In a small bowl, beat three eggs until fluffy (you may omit one of the yolks, if you wish), and season the beaten eggs with salt, pepper, and a pinch of nutmeg. Pour the eggs into the pan, and stir rapidly until they start to coagulate. Evenly spread a portion of the cooked spinach over the omelette and continue to cook about three-and-a-half minutes. When done, the bottom should be very lightly browned and the inside completely set. Roll the omelette onto a plate and let it cool. Repeat the process for each omelette. When you are done, wrap the omelettes separately and place them in a picnic container to transport them.

PLATEAU DES FROMAGES: Select several creamy dessert cheeses that can be spread easily.

Try Brie, Roquefort, Camembert, or St-André. For a true touch of Provence, look for a Banon goat cheese wrapped in chestnut leaves and marinated in eau-de-vie. If this is not available, you can substitute a fresh French goat cheese. Spread the cheese on slices of the *ficelles*.

CROISSANTS AUX AMANDES: Aix — the almond center of France — is noted for its *calissons*, small diamond-sized cakes of almond paste and candied melon under a white sugary crust. These can be difficult to find and are hard to make, so shop instead for fresh almond croissants, a traditional French breakfast pastry.

Staging Your Breakfast Picnic

Plan your breakfast picnic and morning walk for a warm summer day. Everyone should be ready to leave early so you'll arrive at your picnic spot while the day is still cool. When you've found your ideal location, spread a colorful cloth and lay out the prosciutto and melon for your guests. Open the wine — it should have just a touch of chill, about the same temperature as the flesh of the melon. Follow the melon with the omelettes and croissants, but save some wine for the cheeses, which you can enjoy as a final course after your morning stroll.

Before the sun gets too hot, set off together or separately to explore the natural wonders of your surroundings. When you return to your picnic site, nibble on the cheeses and *ficelles*, and indulge in another small glass of sweet wine. By the time you're ready to leave, the day will still be young. You'll have plenty of time for a stop at an outdoor cafe to linger over strong coffee and watch the passersby.

Wedged between the white, windy peaks of Mt. Ventoux to the north, and the Luberon Range to the south, is the high arid plateau of the Vaucluse. It is a patchwork of frugal sheep pastures, tenacious vineyards, and perfumed fields of lavender stretching between hilltop villages and severe rocky gorges. Beneath these rugged highlands, the seasonal rains disappear into a maze of underground rivers, then reemerge in frothy torrents from the deep cavern of the Vaucluse Fountain to cascade into the Sorgue.

Autumn Hunters' Lunch on the Vaucluse Plateau

Fall is the time of the *vendange*, the annual grape harvest. The vines begin to change from green to rust in the autumnal chill, and a patina of blue haze hovers over the villages. The slopes of the Luberon begin to quake with hunters and barking dogs, who stalk boar, rabbit, and game birds.

As the year grows colder, a different hunt takes place on Mt. Ventoux. These hunters are more furtive, accompanied by dogs and pet pigs to sniff out the musky odor of the rare Vaucluse truffle, called the "black diamond" of Provence. The delectable fungus will be sold for a king's ransom at the Carpentras truffle market before winding up on the menus of the best chefs in France. At midday the searchers pause for a traditional hunter's lunch — a campfire feast worthy of the delectable treasures that they seek.

Pâté with Truffles and Pain de Campagne *(peasant bread)*

Lapin en Papillote *(rabbit cooked in foil)*

Salade Frisée et Chèvre à l'Huile *(curly endive salad with marinated goat cheese)*

Côtes du Luberon and Côtes de Ventoux *(red wines of the region)*

Poached Spiced Pears

Preparing Your Hunters' Lunch

Unless you are planning a campfire to cook the meat, most of the picnic is prepared in advance. Shop the day before for the meat, pâté, produce, wine, breads, and marinated goat cheese. The poached pears are made the night before. In the morning, the rabbit is cooked and thin slices of baguette are toasted to accompany the salad.

PÂTÉ: Begin your picnic with pâté or terrine of wild game, which you can find at a gourmet grocer. Look for a *pâté truffée* — one laced with dark bits of truffle that impart an aromatic woodsy flavor. If a wild game pâté is unavailable, purchase about twelve ounces of chicken liver pâté marinated in Cognac and lightly perfumed with Provençal spices. Serve the pâté with slices of *pain de campagne*, a round hardy peasant bread made with rye or whole-wheat flours.

LAPIN EN PAPILLOTE: During the hunting season, the outdoor markets in France are filled with brightly colored game birds, hare, wild boar, and stag. While such delicacies may be less abundant where you live, neighborhood butchers and specialty stores often stock fresh rabbit (chicken may be substituted). Buy one rabbit (or four whole chicken breasts, skinned) for four people. Have the butcher cut the rabbit in half lengthwise, and then cut each half into two sections.

Prepare the rabbit the morning of your picnic. Rinse the meat in cold water and wipe dry. Brush each section with olive oil, and roll the pieces in a mixture of fresh rosemary leaves, minced garlic, chopped fresh parsley, salt, and pepper. Encircle each piece with a strip of bacon and wrap

the pieces individually in aluminum foil. Be sure the seams are carefully sealed so the cooking liquids do not leak.

If you have a campfire, place the packets on a grill over coals for thirty minutes, turning several times. If you are cooking at home, place the packets on a baking sheet and bake for forty minutes in a preheated 375 degree oven. Transfer the wrapped meats to a picnic container. Let your guests unwrap their own portions.

SALADE FRISÉE ET CHÈVRE À L'HUILE: *Chèvre à l'huile*, or marinated goat cheese, can be found in gourmet stores. Pack your picnic basket with a jar containing four small round goat cheeses that have been marinated in olive oil; the washed and dried leaves from two heads of curly endive; sixteen thin slices of baguette, toasted and wrapped in paper; and a jar of vinaigrette made from one tablespoon of red wine vinegar, three tablespoons of olive oil, one tablespoon of the oil marinade from the cheeses, one-half teaspoon of Dijon mustard, and salt and pepper.

At the picnic site, shred the endive into a salad bowl and toss with vinaigrette. Serve the salad on individual plates. Top each salad with a crumbled goat cheese and slices of toasted baguette. If you have a campfire, cut the cheese rounds into quarters, place them on slices of baguette, and grill lightly to heat the cheese and toast the bread. Top the salad with the warm cheese croûtons.

CÔTES DU LUBERON AND CÔTES DU VENTOUX: These red wines from the Vaucluse region are rustic, light, and fruity, with a relatively high alcoholic content. Buy two bottles — one to drink with the pâté and the rabbit, the other to use for poaching the pears. Serve these wines cool but not chilled.

POACHED SPICED PEARS: This cool, spicy dessert blends the young, fruity wine of the *vendange* with the autumn pear harvest. If wines from the Vaucluse are not available, substitute a Beaujolais (the *Nouveau* arrives in mid-November).

Prepare the pears the night before your picnic so they will be thoroughly chilled. Peel and core four pears from the bottom, leaving them whole with the stem protruding. Place the fruit in a non-aluminum saucepan and cover with three fourths of a bottle of wine, one-half cup of sugar, one cinnamon stick, two whole cloves, four peppercorns, and a sprinkling of grated orange and lemon zests. Simmer, covered, for about twenty-five minutes, or until the pears are tender. Remove the pears to a leakproof container and set aside. Reduce the remaining liquid to a syrup and pour over the pears. Seal the container and refrigerate overnight.

Staging Your Hunter's Lunch

Indian summer comes after the first frost. The air is clear and crisp, the leaves are turning, and it's warm only in direct sunlight. Autumn picnickers bundle in flannel shirts, sweaters, and jackets against the chill of late afternoon. A crackling wood fire creates a warming centerpiece for a bracing hunters' lunch.

To celebrate the hunting season — which is, after all, merely an excuse to enjoy the out-of-doors with good friends — it is important to have something to hunt. Why not hunt for the last of the wild herbs growing in tufts among the rocks? Or, if it has rained recently, bring a field guide and search for mushrooms in the woods — a time-honored excuse for a picnic in Provence.

PICTURE CREDITS

Grateful acknowledgment is made for permission to reproduce the following works of art
by Vincent van Gogh:

Page 5: *La Meridienne (The Siesta).* Paris, Musee d'Orsay.

Page 19: *View of Arles with Irises.* Amsterdam, Rijksmuseum Vincent van Gogh.

Page 25: *Landscape at St. Remy.* Copenhagen, Ny Carlsberg Glyptotek. Scala/Art Resource, N.Y.

Page 31: *Starry Night Over the Rhone,* 1888. Paris, Musee d'Orsay. Giraudon/Art Resource, N.Y.

Page 37: *Les Roulottes (Gypsy Encampment).* Paris, Musee d'Orsay. Giraudon/Art Resource, N.Y.

Page 43: *Pollard Willows and Setting Sun,* 1888. Otterloo, Kroller Muller Museum.

Page 49: *Boats on the Beach.* Amsterdam, Rijksmuseum Vincent van Gogh.

Page 55: *Wheatfield with Cypress.* The National Gallery, London.

Page 61: *The Mulberry Tree,* 1889. Norton Simon Art Foundation.